OUR Powerful Helper

Relying on God's Strength

**Six Studies for Groups or Individuals
with Notes for Leaders**

Marshall Shelley
Foreword by J. I. Packer

Inter-Varsity Press

INTER-VARSITY PRESS
38 De Montfort Street, Leicester LE1 7GP, England

OUR POWERFUL HELPER: *Relying on God's Strength*

First published in the USA by Zondervan Publishing House in 1994

First British edition 1995

British Library Cataloguing in Publication Data

A catalogue record for this book is available from the British Library.

ISBN 0-85111-352-4

Typeset and printed in the United States of America

Inter-Varsity Press is the book-publishing division of the Universities and Colleges Christian Fellowship (formerly the Inter-Varsity Fellowship), a student movement linking Christian Unions in universities and colleges throughout the United Kingdom and the Republic of Ireland and a member movement of the International Fellowship of Evangelical Students. For information about local and national activities write to UCCF, 38 De Montfort Street, Leicester LE1 7GP.

95 96 97 98 99 00 /DP/ 6 5 4 3 2 1

Contents

Foreword

One big difference between our current culture and that of a century ago is that the Victorians saw life in terms of roles, while we see it in terms of relationships. Real life, we say, is a matter of relationships, for roles minimize personal involvement while relationships maximize it.

In saying this, we speak more Christian truth than perhaps we realize. For real life according to the Bible means relating not just to other people but also to the personal God who made us. We live and move and exist in him, and it is both scandalous and impoverishing when we ignore him.

Who is he? The startling truth is that he is a *society*. The Father, Son, and Holy Spirit share with each other an intimate and loving relationship. Yet in the unity of their interpersonal life, they constitute a single divine being. God is they, a society and a team, and they are he, the only God there is.

A mystery? An inexplicable reality? Yes, but a life-giving one. It is our privilege not simply to acknowledge the truth of the Trinity but also to enter into Spirit-sustained relationship with the Father and the Son—a relationship which from one standpoint is *eternal life*, and from another is *knowing God*.

Knowing people involves, first, knowing facts about them and, second, making their acquaintance. How deep our relationship goes depends on how much empathy we have, how many concerns and interests we share, and how much we seek to exalt the one we love. It is the same with knowing God.

The Bible is God's communication to all who hear or read it. Through its varied contents the Triune Lord tells us about himself and calls us to himself. A proper understanding of the Bible will focus at every point on both the information about God and the invitation to know him.

Knowing God Bible Studies are designed to help you achieve this focus. I heartily recommend them. They generate vision, insight, wisdom, and devotion in equal quantities. Use them and you will be blessed.

J. I. Packer

Knowing God Bible Studies

Every Christian desires a deeper, more personal relationship with God. We long to know him better, to feel his presence, and to experience his power in our lives. Jesus himself tells us, "This is eternal life: that they may know you, the only true God, and Jesus Christ, whom you have sent" (John 17:3).

Knowing God Bible Studies can help you build greater intimacy with God. The series explores who God is and how you can know him better. Each guide focuses on a specific attribute of God, such as his love, his faithfulness, or his mercy. The studies are warm and practical and personal—yet they are firmly grounded in Scripture.

The Knowing God series has been field tested in churches across America, representing a wide variety of denominations. This time-intensive process ensures that the guides have solid biblical content, consistent quality, easy-to-use formats, and helpful leader's notes.

Knowing God Bible Studies are designed to be flexible. You can use the guides in any order that is best for you or your group. They are ideal for Sunday-school classes, small groups, one-on-one relationships, or as materials for your quiet times.

Because each guide contains only six studies, you can easily explore more than one attribute of God. In a Sunday-school class, any two guides can be combined for a quarter (twelve weeks), or the entire series can be covered in a year.

Each study deliberately focuses on a limited number of passages, usually only one or two. That allows you to see each passage in its context, avoiding the temptation of prooftexting and the frustration of "Bible hopscotch" (jumping from verse to verse). If you would like to look up additional passages, a Bible concordance will give the most help.

Knowing God Bible Studies help you *discover* what the Bible says rather than simply *telling* you the answers. The questions encourage you to think and to explore options rather than merely to fill in the blanks with one-word answers.

Leader's notes are provided in the back of each guide. They show how to lead a group discussion, provide additional information on questions, and suggest ways to deal with problems that may come up in the discussion. With such helps, someone with little or no experience can lead an effective study.

SUGGESTIONS FOR INDIVIDUAL STUDY

1. Begin each study with prayer. Ask God to help you understand the passage and to apply it to your life.

2. A good modern translation, such as the *New International Version*, the *New American Standard Bible*, or the *New Revised Standard Version*, will give you the most help. Questions in this guide, however, are based on the *New International Version*.

3. Read and reread the passage(s). You must know what the passage says before you can understand what it means and how it applies to you.

4. Write your answers in the space provided in the study guide. This will help you to clearly express your understanding of the passage.

5. Keep a Bible dictionary handy. Use it to look up any unfamiliar words, names, or places.

1. Come to the study prepared. Careful preparation will greatly enrich your time in group discussion.

2. Be willing to join in the discussion. The leader of the group will not be lecturing but will encourage people to discuss what they have learned in the passage. Plan to share what God has taught you in your individual study.

3. Stick to the passage being studied. Base your answers on the verses being discussed rather than on outside authorities such as commentaries or your favorite author or speaker.

4. Try to be sensitive to the other members of the group. Listen attentively when they speak, and be affirming whenever you can. This will encourage more hesitant members of the group to participate.

5. Be careful not to dominate the discussion. By all means participate! But allow others to have equal time.

6. If you are the discussion leader, you will find additional suggestions and helpful ideas in the leader's notes at the back of the guide.

Introducing Our Powerful Helper

This series of studies was born out of an intense personal search to understand the ways of God, and to learn how we could lean on him for strength.

In March 1990 our daughter Mandy was born. Amid the happiness surrounding her successful birth, the doctors told us she had microcephaly (small brain). We'd never heard the term before. Little did we know how Mandy's condition would affect our lives.

In Mandy's case, the microcephaly produced severe and profound retardation. She was never able to crawl, to sit up, to utter any words, to use her hands to grasp. She suffered frequent seizures. We never knew if she could see or hear. The only communication we had with her was when we would give her a bath—occasionally she would visibly relax in the warm water. Eventually she was unable to swallow effectively enough to sustain herself, so she had to be fed through a tube surgically implanted into her stomach.

As my wife, Susan, and I cared for her, we wondered about God's purposes. And many of our friends asked us the questions we were asking ourselves: Why would God allow—no, *assign*— such a severe condition to a child? (There was no known cause for Mandy's microcephaly, except for God's design.) What is her future? Where does the strength come from to care for her?

The only answers that came close to satisfying our confusion centered around God's unexplainable will, the hope of the resurrection, and providing his body, the church, to embody his love and care.

Then in November 1991 our son Toby was born. We learned during the pregnancy that he had a chromosomal abnormality called Trisomy 13, a condition the doctors had described as "incompatible with life." He lived two minutes. He spent his entire earthly life on Susan's chest.

Along with the waves of grief, the questions again swept over us: What kind of God creates a child to live two minutes? Genetic tests indicated no relationship between Mandy's condition and Toby's. Both cases were "flukes," design flaws in nature. We reeled under the sadness. Three months later, in February 1992, we were hit again when Mandy developed a pneumonia that her body didn't have the strength to shake. After eight days in the hospital, she died. Even though, as Christians, we were convinced Mandy was in heaven with Jesus, we missed her deeply. For two years our lives had revolved around her. Now our house, our arms, our laps, seemed so empty.

This study guide was written within a year of our children's deaths. It was no academic exercise. It was part of our desperate turning to Scripture to discover how God gives strength to his people in difficult times. These six studies focus on six sections of the Bible that offered us fresh glimpses of how God works.

I trust that you will find, as we did, that God does provide comfort when you need it most, and the power to persevere.

Marshall Shelley

1

Power in Weakness

2 Corinthians 12:1-10

Someone has observed, "Personality has the power to open doors, but it takes character to keep them open." Another has said, "You fall in love with a personality, but you have to live with a character."

It's interesting to think about the difference between personality and character—especially your own. Many people long to have "personality," which usually means an outward style that people find attractive. Television features "personalities," often people who are famous only for having a face that has appeared in the media. It is significant that the word *persona* (from which *personality* comes) originally meant a mask or disguise an actor would wear on stage.

Character goes deeper. It is what you are when no one is looking. It is what your life stands for and what values you live by. It takes longer for character to be revealed, but character is what shows when life gets tough.

This study may not help you become a charming personality, but it points the way to becoming a person of character.

1. Who is the strongest character you've known? What made him or her that way?

2. Read 2 Corinthians 12:1–10. In verses 1–6, Paul refers to a mystical experience that words cannot describe. He doesn't name himself as the one involved, but "a man in Christ" probably refers to Paul. Why do you think he is reluctant to talk about such an experience?

3. What do such unexplainable experiences do for the person experiencing them?

4. What, if anything, do they do for people who hear about them?

5. Have you ever had an experience you can't explain, feel inadequate to describe, but in which you encountered the presence of God? What *can* you say about it?

6. In verses 7–8, Paul refers to a chronic and debilitating "thorn in the flesh." No one knows for sure what it was, but what kinds of things might Paul be referring to?

Why would such a condition prevent conceit?

7. Paul says he "delights" in weakness, insults, and hardships. (Note some of the things he lists in 2 Corinthians 11:24–33.) What do these things reveal about Paul? About God?

8. How is God's power "made perfect" in weakness?

9. Whom do you respect more—someone who has enjoyed unbroken success, or someone who has endured pain, sorrow, and defeat? Why?

10. In the 1600's, Sebastian Valfre observed, "When it is all over, you will not regret having suffered; rather you will regret having suffered so little and suffered that little so badly." What do you think he meant?

How do you feel about his statement?

11. In today's world, what kinds of weaknesses are people willing to talk about openly?

What is good about this? What are the dangers?

12. What kinds of weaknesses are still hard to be open about?

How is God's power "made perfect" in those kinds of things, too?

Memory Verse

My grace is sufficient for you, for my power is made perfect in weakness.

2 Corinthians 12:9

BETWEEN STUDIES

What are your weaknesses—physical, relational, spiritual, emotional, financial, mental? What recurring pain do you feel? After you've listed them, consider: How might God's power be working in them right now? How might God's power be working through them for the future?

2

The Blazing Furnace

Daniel 3

A fter a church service, a man came up to the pastor and said, "This is the first time I've been in a church for years. My marriage is falling apart. My business is on the brink of failure. Can you help me?"

The pastor could have offered some thoughts on marriage enrichment or suggested a seminar on business principles, but he didn't. He addressed the real issue. "It sounds like you need an invisible means of support," he said. "Yeah, that's it," the man replied. "That's *exactly* what I need." The pastor introduced the man to Jesus Christ, to a new way of life based on trusting God for salvation and for dealing effectively with the overwhelming situations of life.

When we place our faith in Christ, life does not suddenly grow calm. We need strength more than ever. But we need to learn how God's strength comes to us.

1. When have you experienced intense heat (whether emotional or thermal)?

2. Read Daniel 3. What different kinds of heat did the three young men experience?

3. King Nebuchadnezzar called for a nation-wide demonstration of allegiance (vv. 1–6). Why do you think he wanted such a public display of unity?

4. Have you ever been in a situation where the one in charge, like Nebuchadnezzar, expected everyone to "bow and scrape" to his demands? What are the dangers of such situations?

5. Why do you think the extensive list of officials ("satraps, prefects, governors, advisers, treasurers, judges, magistrates, and all the other provincial officials") is repeated (vv. 2–3)?

6. What irony is there in these highly placed individuals "falling down and worshiping an image of gold" (v. 5)?

7. What do you make of the fact that the king didn't know anyone had refused to worship the image until the three men were turned in by their accusers?

8. How did the accusers twist the facts, putting the three men in the worst possible light (vv. 8–12)?

9. Why do you think Shadrach, Meshach, and Abednego chose civil disobedience rather than participating in this national celebration?

10. They told the king that whether or not their God saved them, they would not serve his gods (v. 18). Does that indicate weak faith or strong faith? Why?

11. Some people think living by faith means to "look on the bright side." What's the difference between wishful thinking and the kind of faith these three men showed?

12. Who might the fourth man (v. 25) have been?

What does it say to you that he showed up in the fire, rather than rescuing them earlier?

13. The story ends happily with Nebuchadnezzar officially sanctioning worship of the God of Shadrach, Meshach, and Abednego, and giving favors to the three men. In honoring them, why do you think he mentions that they "defied the king"?

What does that say about the king?

14. Why would the king want to have such people in his service?

Memory Verse

If we are thrown into the blazing furnace, the God we serve is able to save us from it . . . but even if he does not, we want you to know, O king, that we will not serve your gods or worship the image of gold you have set up.

Daniel 3:17–18

▬▬ BETWEEN STUDIES ▬▬

Living by faith doesn't always guarantee that we will be rescued from danger or from difficult situations. Read Hebrews 11 for a fuller definition of faith. That chapter also lists several people who are described as having faith. What is similar about their faith and that of Shadrach, Meshach, and Abednego?

3

Chariots of Fire

2 Kings 6:8-23

Sometimes the best gifts are those we least expect, maybe even gifts we didn't think we wanted—until we saw their true value.

Consider the following prayer from an unknown Confederate soldier during the Civil War:

> I asked God for strength that I might achieve. I was made weak that I might learn humbly to obey. I asked God for health that I might do greater things. I was given infirmity that I might do better things. I asked for riches that I might be happy. I was given poverty that I might be wise. I asked for power that I might have the praise of men. I was given weakness that I might see the need of God. I asked for all things that I might enjoy life. I was given life that I might enjoy all things. I got nothing that I asked for but everything I had hoped for. Almost despite myself my unspoken prayers were answered. I am among all men most richly blessed.

This man was given eyes to see what he'd been unable to see before. This is a gift we too must seek if we are to experience God's strength.

1. Describe one time when you saw a "sight for sore eyes"? (Either a beautiful or welcome sight that renewed your strength.)

2. Read 2 Kings 6:8–23. When Elisha repeatedly informed Israel's king about the enemy's troop movements (vv. 8–11), the king of Aram (today's Syria) accused his staff of harboring a traitor. Why do you think he made this assumption?

3. How do you suppose the Syrian officers knew that Elisha was the source of Israel's military intelligence?

4. Have you ever known someone who could predict another person's behavior—who understood how someone would react? How does a person know such things?

5. The covert operation continues with the Syrian king learning of Elisha's whereabouts (vv. 13–14). Do you see anything ironic about the Syrians trying to sneak up on Elisha? Explain.

6. After seeing they were surrounded, how do you think Elisha's servant felt about being told, "Don't be afraid" (v. 16)?

How would you have felt?

7. When first told that "those who are with us are more than those who are with them," what would have been your reaction?

8. After seeing "the hills full of horses and chariots of fire," suddenly the servant realized, "There's more here than meets the eye." What does such an awareness do for you when you're in a difficult situation?

9. Sometimes seeing "the big picture" means we recognize the spiritual realities surrounding our specific circumstances. Read the statement above written by the unknown Confederate soldier. What was the difference between his requests and the answers he got?

10. When has God given you, not what you asked for, but what you truly needed and longed for?

11. God provides a surprising (and humane) form of deliverance for the Syrians (vv. 18–23). Why do you think Elisha insisted on treating the Syrians so well?

12. The raids from Aram stopped for a while (v. 23), but the peace was only temporary (v. 24). Even after God's deliverance, more threatening situations will come. How does this fact affect your relationship with God?

Memory Verse

Don't be afraid. . . . Those who are with us are more than those who are with them.

2 Kings 6:16

▌ BETWEEN STUDIES ▌

Read the rest of 2 Kings 6–7. Notice how the anger of Israel turns against Elisha. Why? Why are people of faith resented?

4

God's Invisible Direction

Psalm 23

When was the time you were most afraid? Perhaps it was when you were alone in an unfamiliar part of the city. Or perhaps when your job or your marriage was threatened. Or when serious illness put your health (or your child's health) in danger. Whatever the cause, fear can enter our lives uninvited and when we least expect it.

God has provided a means of facing our fears. One of the most familiar passages in the Bible deals with our daily dependence on God—turning to him in times of both fear and refreshment.

As you reread Psalm 23, think about whether your thoughts have been turned toward God more intensely in times of fear, or in times of refreshment.

1. Describe one time when you were really afraid.

Describe one time when you really felt refreshed.

2. Read Psalm 23. Two main word-pictures are used to describe God in this psalm: a shepherd (vv. 1–4) and the host (vv. 5–6). What do these two have in common?

How are they different?

3. Notice at least four things the shepherd does for the sheep (vv. 1–3). How do each of those phrases apply not just to sheep but to people?

4. Think of one leader you've known or observed that you really respect. How is he or she like this good shepherd?

5. Verse 4 suddenly changes the mood. Why do you think that David includes this darker picture?

6. How do the words "valley of the shadow of death" (v. 4) describe what's really involved when you experience fear?

7. Why does David "fear no evil" and find "comfort" in the dark valley?

How have you experienced God's comforting presence in dark times?

8. What are at least four things God, as the host, does for his guests (vv. 5-6)?

Which of those "guest services" do you most appreciate?

9. How can you eat "in the presence of enemies"? Wouldn't that make you lose your appetite? (See Leader's Notes in the back of the book.)

10. Now, after considering each line of Psalm 23, read it through again as a whole. What impresses you now about this description of God's character?

Memory Verse

Even though I walk through the valley of the shadow of death, I will fear no evil, for you are with me; your rod and your staff, they comfort me.

Psalm 23:4

BETWEEN STUDIES

Put your life journey on a chart. On a piece of paper, number across the bottom the years to represent your age (zero to 23, 39, or whatever). Graph the highs and the lows over the years. Write in the key events. What were the spiritual peaks? The emotional valleys? As you review the chart, can you see times when the Good Shepherd did for you some of the things David describes in Psalm 23?

David uses the word-pictures of shepherd and host to describe God. What other images from your own experiences would you use to describe his relationship to you?

5

God's Unpredictable Justice

Habakkuk 1-3

Have you ever felt like arguing with God? Have you ever wanted to say, "If you're in control, why do bad guys win and nice guys finish last?" If you have, then you and Habakkuk have something in common.

Habakkuk, whose name may mean "wrestler," grappled with God about questions we still ask: How can a just God ignore injustice? Why doesn't he do more to prevent evil? And how can a good God use evil to accomplish his purposes?

Habakkuk struggled to understand how God works, but in the end he became convinced that he could trust God no matter how bleak or confusing the present circumstances appeared to be.

1. Agree or disagree: "If God is fair, life will be fair." Explain.

2. Read Habakkuk 1:1–4. What contemporary events give you the same kinds of feelings that Habakkuk was expressing?

3. Do you think God was ignoring Habakkuk's prayers (1:2)? Why?

4. Read Habakkuk 1:5–2:1. What was surprising about God's answer to Habakkuk's complaint?

5. Was Habakkuk accurate in his observation (1:13) that God was employing evil to do good? Explain.

6. Have you ever argued with God? Over what?

7. Where does Habakkuk position himself (2:1), and what does this tell you about his expectations of God?

8. Is arguing with God a good idea? Why or why not?

9. In uncertain times, what does it means for a righteous person to live by faith (2:4)?

10. What does it mean that God "is in his holy temple" (2:20)?

11. What does silence before God communicate?

12. Read Habakkuk 3. The prophet remembers what he has heard about God's mighty deeds—especially during the Exodus (vv. 2-15). What portrait of God emerges from verses 3–15?

Why does Habakkuk want God to renew such deeds in his own day (v. 2)?

13. While he waits patiently for "the day of calamity" and a ruined economy (vv. 16-17), how was Habakkuk able to find hope and joy in the Lord (v. 18)?

14. How can knowing God is sovereign (in control) give you hope and joy in troubled times?

Memory Verse

For the earth will be filled with the knowledge of the glory of the LORD, as the waters cover the sea.

Habakkuk 2:14

■ BETWEEN STUDIES ■

Following Habakkuk's example in chapter 1, make your own list of "complaints." Be specific about the ways injustice and cruelty are seen in your world. Then write your own version of chapter 2 of Habakkuk. What do you think God would say about those on your list who are doing the evil? Finally, after considering both your complaints and God's character, describe your own response to God, as Habakkuk did in chapter 3.

6

Going Right to the Top

Luke 11:1-13

Writer A. W. Tozer once described people of faith this way:

> A real Christian is an odd number, anyway. He feels supreme love for One whom he has never seen; talks familiarly every day to Someone he cannot see; expects to go to heaven on the virtue of Another; empties himself in order to be full; admits he is wrong so he can be declared right; goes down in order to get up; is strongest when he is weakest. . . . He dies so he can live; forsakes in order to have; gives away so he can keep; sees the invisible; hears the inaudible; and knows that which passeth knowledge. Sometimes it seems that God enjoys turning things upside down. But one direction is very clear: he invites us to talk to him directly. Through prayer, we can go right to the top.

1. How did you learn to pray?

2. Read Luke 11:1–13, where Jesus teaches the disciples to pray. What are some reasons the disciples might have wanted to learn to pray?

What drives your interest in prayer?

3. If you had been raised in a Jewish culture that dared not speak the holy name of God (for fear of breaking the third of the Ten Commandments, Ex. 20:7), how would you respond when Jesus told you to call God "Father" (v. 2)?

4. How are your prayers affected if you start by remembering that God is holy?

5. When you pray for God's kingdom to come, what are you really praying for?

6. What does praying for "daily bread" (v. 3) mean for people who keep several days' supply of food in their refrigerator?

7. Why do you suppose Jesus links our sins being forgiven with our forgiving those who sin against us (v. 4)?

8. Think of someone who has wronged you. How will God deal with you if he treats you as you treat that person?

9. Think about the temptations you struggle with. Do they take you by surprise, or do you walk into them knowingly? Explain.

10. Jesus' teaching about prayer continues with a story (vv. 5–8). What's the point? That God needs to be nagged? That he's just the opposite—quick to respond? Or something else?

11. What was something you really wanted but had to wait for?

Do you now see any reason why God allowed you to wait?

12. What does persistence in prayer do for the person praying?

13. Jesus says the truly good gift God wants to give is the Holy Spirit (v. 13). Why is that gift better than the standard list of requests we are inclined to present?

Memory Verse

If you then, though you are evil, know how to give good gifts to your children, how much more will your Father in heaven give the Holy Spirit to those who ask him!

Luke 11:13

BETWEEN STUDIES

Now that you have completed this series of studies, summarize the ways God provides strength for his people. What are the various means in his repertoire? How can you depend on God's help in a situation you are currently facing?

Leader's Notes

Leading a Bible discussion—especially for the first time—can make you feel both nervous and excited. If you are nervous, realize that you are in good company. Many biblical leaders, such as Moses, Joshua, and the apostle Paul, felt nervous and inadequate to lead others (see, for example, 1 Cor. 2:3). Yet God's grace was sufficient for them, just as it will be for you.

Some excitement is also natural. Your leadership is a gift to the others in the group. Keep in mind, however, that other group members also share responsibility for the group. Your role is simply to stimulate discussion by asking questions and encouraging people to respond. The suggestions listed below can help you to be an effective leader.

PREPARING TO LEAD

1. Ask God to help you understand and apply the passage to your own life. Unless that happens, you will not be prepared to lead others.

2. Carefully work through each question in the study guide. Meditate and reflect on the passage as you formulate your answers.

3. Familiarize yourself with the leader's notes for the study. These will help you understand the purpose of the study

and will provide valuable information about the questions in the study.

4. Pray for the various members of the group. Ask God to use these studies to make you better disciples of Jesus Christ.

5. Before the first meeting, make sure each person has a study guide. Encourage them to prepare beforehand for each study.

LEADING THE STUDY

1. Begin the study on time. If people realize that the study begins on schedule, they will work harder to arrive on time.

2. At the beginning of your first time together, explain that these studies are designed to be discussions, not lectures. Encourage everyone to participate, but realize that some may be hesitant to speak during the first few sessions.

3. Read the introductory paragraph at the beginning of the discussion. This will orient the group to the passage being studied.

4. Read the passage aloud. You may choose to do this yourself, or you might ask for volunteers.

5. The questions in the guide are designed to be used just as they are written. If you wish, you may simply read each one aloud to the group. Or you may prefer to express them in your own words. Unnecessary rewording of the questions, however, is not recommended.

6. Don't be afraid of silence. People in the group may need time to think before responding.

7. Avoid answering your own questions. If necessary, rephrase a question until it is clearly understood. Even an eager group will quickly become passive and silent if they think the leader will do most of the talking.

8. Encourage more than one answer to each question. Ask, "What do the rest of you think?" or "Anyone else?" until several people have had a chance to respond.

9. Try to be affirming whenever possible. Let people know you appreciate their insights into the passage.

10. Never reject an answer. If it is clearly wrong, ask, "Which verse led you to that conclusion?" Or let the group handle the problem by asking them what they think about the question.

11. Avoid going off on tangents. If people wander off course, gently bring them back to the passage being considered.

12. Conclude your time together with conversational prayer. Ask God to help you apply those things that you learned in the study.

13. End on time. This will be easier if you control the pace of the discussion by not spending too much time on some questions or too little on others.

Many more suggestions and helps are found in the book *Leading Bible Discussions* (InterVarsity Press). Reading it would be well worth your time.

STUDY ONE — *Power in Weakness*
2 CORINTHIANS 12:1–10

Purpose: To discover how God's power is made perfect in weakness, and to point the way to becoming a person of character.

Question 1 Every study begins with a "warm-up question," which is discussed *before* reading the passage. A warm-up question is designed to do three things.

First, it helps to break the ice. Because a warm-up question doesn't require any knowledge of the passage or any special preparation, it can get people talking and can help them to feel more comfortable with each other.

Second, a warm-up question can motivate people to study the passage at hand. At the beginning of the study, people in the group aren't necessarily ready to jump into the world of the Bible. Their minds may be on other things (their kids, a problem at work, an upcoming meeting) that have nothing to do with the study. A warm-up question can capture their interest and draw them into the discussion by raising important issues related to the study. The question becomes a bridge between their personal lives and the answers found in Scripture.

Third, a good warm-up question can reveal where people's thoughts or feelings need to be transformed by Scripture. That is why it is important to ask the warm-up question *before* reading the passage. The passage might inhibit the spontaneous, honest answers people might have given, because they feel compelled to give biblical answers. The warm-up question allows them to compare their personal thoughts and feelings with what they later discover in Scripture.

Question 2 We don't know for sure when this vision happened in Paul's life. It may have been when he was near death (Acts 14:19–20). Or it may have been a dream or a supernatural experience. Whatever it was, Paul recognizes that people will find it hard to believe.

Question 3 Among other things, they certainly are reminded that there is another world beyond this physical universe, and that much of our life is unexplainable.

Question 5 Polls of the American people indicate that 33 percent say they have had "a religious experience, an insight, or awakening that changed the course of my life." Whether a religious conversion, a close call in an automobile accident, a life-threatening illness, or a mystical experience, people often are convinced that God has communicated to them.

Question 6 Among the possibilities suggested for Paul's thorn in the flesh: epilepsy, impaired vision, malaria, migraines, critical opposition, temptations, or spiritual pride. Perhaps it is best that we do not know the precise nature of Paul's "thorn" because those with other weaknesses can also be encouraged to rely on God's strength.

STUDY TWO

The Blazing Furnace
DANIEL 3

Purpose: To learn how God's strength comes to us when life turns up the heat.

Question 3 "'King Nebuchadrezzar made an image of gold' and 'set it up'. These words form a refrain through the first half of the chapter (verses 1–18). The image was intended to be worshipped, but the writer does not call it a god. The fact that all peoples, nations and languages were to fall down and worship it suggests that Nebuchadrezzar intended to unite his kingdom under one religion. It may even be that the image represented himself. Having been told that he was the head of gold [see 2:38], what more natural than to capitalize on the fact and to make the whole image of gold?" (Joyce G. Baldwin, *Daniel*, Tyndale Old Testament Commentaries, ed. D. J. Wiseman [Downers Grove, Ill.: InterVarsity Press, 1978], p. 99).

Question 5 "The exact repetition of the list of officials and of the musical instruments may reflect a Semitic style of rhetoric, but the writer succeeds in achieving a satirical effect which may not have been unintentional. Here are all the great ones of the empire falling flat on their faces before a lifeless obelisk at the sound of a musical medley, controlled by the baton of King Nebuchaddrezzar" (Baldwin, *Daniel*, p. 102).

Question 8 "*Maliciously accused* translates the picturesque expression 'eat the pieces of flesh torn off from someone's body' and so 'to slander'. The accusers are well aware of the circumstances in which these Jews were appointed to office and they resent the king's promotion of foreigners over their heads. Now is their opportunity to gain the favour of the king by revealing treachery" (Baldwin, *Daniel*, pp. 103-4).

Questions 10, 12 The Lord does not promise that he will always deliver us from fiery trials, but he does promise to be with us in the midst of them (see 2 Cor. 1:3–11; 4:7–18; Heb. 13:5–6).

STUDY THREE	*Chariots of Fire*
	2 KINGS 6:8–23

Purpose: To consider why we need to see with the eyes of faith if we are to experience God's strength.

Question 2 The king was suspicious. He had spies everywhere, and relied on them for information. When he discovered Israel had information about his own movements, he naturally assumed a security leak.

Question 3 The king of Aram probably had an informer within the government of Israel.

Question 5 If Elisha knew all their movements previously, he no doubt was aware of their move to capture him.

Question 7 This parallels the truth that Paul utters in the New Testament, "If God is for us, who can be against us?" (Rom. 8:31).

Question 11 Such treatment was the only hope for breaking the cycle of hostility.

STUDY FOUR	**God's Invisible Direction**

God's Invisible Direction
PSALM 23

Purpose: To be encouraged to depend on God in times of fear and refreshment.

Question 6 Tell the group to think about what's required to produce a shadow. How is that similar to what happens when we're afraid or when we face death?

The phrase "valley of the shadow of death" can be translated "the valley as dark as death," meaning the most fearful experiences of life. But the word-picture of a shadow is even more picturesque. In order for there to be a shadow, there must be light, and there must be something blocking that light. Likewise, when we're afraid, it's usually because something appears between us and God's light.

A shadow is also without true substance. Being hit by the shadow of a truck is nothing like being hit by the truck itself. Even though shadows can be fearful, we can take comfort from knowing they ultimately are powerless when God is with us.

Question 7 Think about what a rod and staff do for sheep: a rod is a club to beat off enemies, a staff is a longer stick, usually with a hook on the end, to direct the sheep or to rescue them when they've fallen. Consider how God's rod and staff—his firm direction and the discipline of his Word—can also provide comfort for us.

Question 9 The word picture here refers to a victorious army feasting after a battle, with the captured foes looking on. The enemies, who had been trying to do you harm, are no longer a threat. It's celebration time. The image is of God preparing a victory feast.

God's Unpredictable Justice

HABAKKUK 1–3

Purpose: To realize that we can trust God no matter how bleak or confusing the present circumstances appear to be.

Question 4 An invasion by the Babylonians was a terrifying prospect. When Habakkuk asked God to end the corruption in Judah, he didn't expect God to do it so severely. True, Judah's King, Jehoiakim, and his cronies had grown wealthy by injustice and extortion. They had even enslaved their own people (Jer. 22:13, 17) and arrogantly burned the writings of Jeremiah, another prophet who pled for justice (Jer. 36:23–27). But if Judah was bad, the Babylonians were worse! Habakkuk knew about their sadistic reputation—chariots and horsemen trampling defenders; armies laying siege and starving cities into submission; soldiers torturing and raping, ripping open pregnant women, holding infants by the heels and smashing them against the stone walls. Now this army of destruction was coming toward Judah. And in 597 B.C. they conquered Jerusalem, destroyed the temple, killed the sons of the king before his eyes and then blinded him (2 Kings 25:5–7), and took the people into captivity.

Question 5 So Habbakkuk's corrupt nation was going to be overrun by a vicious invader—this was God's justice? To Habakkuk, the cure seemed worse than the disease. How could a greater wrong correct a bad situation?

Eventually God enlarged Habakkuk's vision. He saw that God is in control even when it appears he is not: "Has not the Lord Almighty determined . . . that the nations exhaust themselves for nothing?" (2:13). God uses people and nations, often without their knowledge, for his good purposes. At times the events seem evil, but God's severity, like a surgeon's scalpel, is working not to hurt but to heal. In a word, yes, God does use evil to do good. But the reason he does is that he's working to transform the tragic circumstances of a fallen world so that good ultimately prevails.

Question 7 Watchmen stood in watchtowers to guard against possible invasion or to watch for messengers. "Ramparts" (2:1) were an embankment of earth beyond the city walls and were the first lines of defense. Habakkuk describes himself as a watchman, waiting and ready for God's answer to his question.

Question 8 Passionate, honest, even angry prayers seem to be a trademark of many spiritual giants of the Bible. Habakkuk wasn't the only one to complain: Moses, Gideon, Elijah, and Job, among others, also questioned and argued with God. God listens with a sympathetic ear when we complain about injustice. Whenever we are jolted by life's unfairness, we should realize that God was bothered by such things long before we were. In fact, injustice would not upset us at all if God had not given us a sense of justice. Where else could we get a sense of right and wrong if not from God?

Because God knows our deepest thoughts, we might as well be honest with him (and ourselves) and admit when we feel outraged or confused. But watch out! God's "answer" may be as perplexing as the problem. God isn't obligated to answer our questions as we'd expect.

God seldom explains himself or his ways completely. Even if he did, we wouldn't have the capacity to comprehend his answers. But God overwhelms us with his power and love. In the end, though we may not know the answers to our questions, we can know him better. Asking hard questions of God forces us to look not just at the answers we want, but at the character of God himself.

Question 9 To trust God, to continue to obey him, to believe he will act, even when circumstances look like he's forgotten—that's what faith is all about.

Question 10 This phrase suggests that even though everything on earth is in shambles, God still reigns. All things are under his control and in his power.

Question 13 Was Habakkuk kidding himself? To rejoice during disaster seems totally inappropriate if you look only at present circumstances. But faith in God adds a new ingredient. Habakkuk learned to look beyond his present troubles to a larger perspective. Faith assures us, just as it did Habakkuk, that our all-powerful God will eventually resolve the trouble we're in, even when things seem hopeless. This isn't denial; it's deferred reality.

<table>
<tr><td>STUDY
SIX</td><td></td></tr>
</table>

Going Right to the Top
LUKE 11:1–13

Purpose: To learn a model of prayer from the Lord himself, and to realize that God invites us to talk to him directly through prayer.

Question 1 Perhaps you learned to pray at your bedside as a child. Perhaps it was through instruction at church. Or perhaps you learned to pray through difficult experiences that drove you to God.

Question 3 Only through Jesus would you have the freedom to address God in such a familiar way. Jesus' model teaches us to pray with a blend of intimacy and awe.

Question 4 In this case, *name* means more than just something we call somebody. It refers to who the person really is. Here God's "name" is his character. And at the core, God is holy, which literally means "set apart"—he is pure, sacred. When we pray, we must remember that his plans for us may be different than our own natural desires.

Question 5 You are praying for God's ruling authority to be recognized here on earth, even as it's already recognized by the inhabitants of heaven.

Question 6 It's easy to forget that every meal, indeed every breath comes from God. Remembering this may tend to simplify our prayers to the essentials, not our ever-expanding list of wants.

Question 7 Someone has said, "When we refuse to forgive, we burn a bridge over which we ourselves will want to cross." Another way of putting it: In God's kingdom, the currency is grace and forgiveness. You can't do business with God unless you accept and use that currency.

Question 10 The story is a contrast parable—showing that God is *not* like the reluctant friend. God is eager to meet our needs. The problem with this interpretation, of course, is that in our experience, not all prayers are quickly answered in the way we've asked. Jesus suggests that if you don't receive what you ask for, it's because God has something better for you. God is eager to give us truly *good* gifts. To rephrase Jesus, "If you ask for a snake—even one you think you'd like to have—God may not oblige, because he knows the fish is better."

Question 12 Too many people pray like little boys who knock at doors and then run away. Persistence in prayer may reveal how strongly we really desire what we're asking for. It can purify motives, it can make us recognize our true dependence on God, and it can make us willing to consider other ways God might meet the need of our heart.